What Good Is a Y?

amicus
readers

1

by Marie Powell

amicus readers

Say Hello to Amicus Readers.

You'll find our helpful dog, Amicus, chasing a ball—to let you know the reading level of a book.

1

Learn to Read

Frequent repetition, high frequency words, and close photo-text matches introduce familiar topics and provide ample support for brand new readers.

2

Read Independently

Some repetition is mixed with varied sentence structures and a select amount of new vocabulary words are introduced with text and photo support.

3

Read to Know More

Interesting facts and engaging art and photos give fluent readers fun books both for reading practice and to learn about new topics.

Amicus Readers are published by Amicus
P.O. Box 1329, Mankato, MN 56002
www.amicuspublishing.us

Library of Congress Cataloging-in-Publication Data

Powell, Marie, 1958-
  What good is a Y? / by Marie Powell.
      pages cm. -- (Vowels)
  Summary: " Beginning readers are introduced to the vowel Y and its sounds and uses, including the oi sound and its use as a consonant."-- Provided by publisher.
  ISBN 978-1-60753-713-7 (library binding)
  ISBN 978-1-60753-817-2 (ebook)
  1. Vowels--Juvenile literature. 2. English language--Vowels--Juvenile literature.
  PE1157.P69448 2015
  428.1'3--dc23
                    2014045797

Photo Credits: Miriam Elizabeth/iStock/Thinkstock, cover; Shutterstock Images, 1, 4-5, 16 (top left), 16 (bottom right); Ewa Studio/Shutterstock Images, 3; Sergey Novikov/Shutterstock Images, 7, 16 (top right); iStockphoto, 8, 16 (bottom left); Alice Kirichenko/Shutterstock Images, 11; Wavebreakmedia/Thinkstock, 12-13; Warren Goldswain/Shutterstock Images, 15

Produced for Amicus by The Peterson Publishing Company and Red Line Editorial.

Editor Jenna Gleisner
Designer Craig Hinton

Printed in Malaysia
10 9 8 7 6 5 4 3 2 1

What good is a Y? Y is a consonant. Y can also be a vowel, like A, E, I, O, and U. What vowel sounds does Y make?

Y can have a long I sound.
My friend and I fly
our kites.

4

Y can have a short I sound. We bicycle to the park. We pass the gym.

<u>Y</u> can have a long E sound. Flying a kite can be trick<u>y</u> when it is ver<u>y</u> wind<u>y</u>.

Y and A together make a long A sound. Tod**ay** the wind m**ay** blow my kite aw**ay**.

Y and O together can make an oi sound. Out of all of my t**oy**s, I enj**oy** my kite the most.

Y can start a word.
"You can see my yellow
kite up high!" yells Yan.
Y can make all kinds
of words.

Vowel: Y

Which <u>Y</u> words have a long <u>I</u> sound?

Which <u>Y</u> words have a short <u>I</u> sound?

Which <u>Y</u> words have a long <u>E</u> sound?

fly

bicycle

windy

gym